Little
ACORN

AUTUMN
PUBLISHING

Published in 2022
First published in the UK by Autumn Publishing
An imprint of Igloo Books Ltd
Cottage Farm, NN6 0BJ, UK
Owned by Bonnier Books
Sveavägen 56, Stockholm, Sweden
www.autumnpublishing.co.uk

0522 004
2 4 6 8 10 9 7 5 3
ISBN 978-1-83852-649-8

Illustrated by Gina Maldonado
Written by Melanie Joyce

Designed by Lee Italiano
Edited by Emily Bruce

Printed and manufactured in China

Little
ACORN

AUTUMN
PUBLISHING

When I was just an acorn,
nobody noticed me.

I watched the world below go by
from high up in my tree.

I nestled under cosy leaves, and sheltered from the rain,

Growing fat and shiny when the sun came out again.

When the summer faded, the leaves
turned golden brown.

"Bye bye, Acorn!"
said the leaves, floating to the ground.

"Wait for me!" I called,
then, ready, steady, jump!

Whee!
I tumbled through the air...

... and landed with a **thump.**

Squirrel was collecting nuts for his winter store.

He hid me carefully away beneath the forest floor.

Underground, everything was snuggly and still.

I waited very patiently for time to pass until...

I felt a sudden change beginning deep inside.
"I'm feeling so peculiar. What's happening?"
I cried.

"You're growing up!" said the worms, all wriggling about.

"When acorns fall into the soil,
at some time they will sprout!"

I giggled as I felt tickly, teeny-tiny shoots,
And, before I knew it, I had sprouted little roots!

I started to stretch up, wiggling left and right...

... reaching up and up till I pushed out into the light.

Warmed by gentle sunbeams,
my little leaves unfurled. I was so
excited to be back out in the world.

As the weeks and months passed by...

...I grew...

...and grew...

...and grew.

Squirrel spotted me and said,

"I've been looking everywhere for you!"

The seasons changed, and so did I,

in sunshine...

... rain...

... and snow.

My branches stretched...

... my trunk grew tall, my roots spread far below.

Among my sturdy branches,
the birds built
cosy nests.

My twigs and leaves made
soft, warm beds for my
feathered guests.

Spiders weaved their sticky
webs, and beetles scurried by.

Squirrels scampered
playfully, and made their
homes up high.

The creatures of the forest had never seen a finer tree.

I wondered, would there ever be another one like me?

Then, one breezy morning, I woke up with a yawn.
I stretched my branches...

... and out jumped...

... a special little...

...acorn!

Every oak tree
starts life as a seed
called an acorn, growing on an
adult tree. The acorn drops off
into the soil, where it sprouts roots.
As the roots grow down, a leafy shoot
sprouts up, growing taller and taller.
The acorn is now a baby tree called a
seedling. It continues to grow bigger
and bigger until it is a new oak tree,
and grows acorns of its own.